The Lap-Reluctant Cat

by Stephanie Bouchard

illustrated by Beth Zyglowicz

Avalonski Press

For Avalon,
my lap-reluctant cat.

Avalonski Press
The Lap-Reluctant Cat
Stephanie Bouchard

Copyright © 2013 by Stephanie Bouchard
All Rights Reserved

Editor: Dale Evva Gelfand
Illustrations: Beth Zyglowicz
Book design: Kevin Callahan,
BNGO Books

All rights reserved.
This book is self-published by the author Stephanie Bouchard under Avalonski Press. No part of this book may be reproduced in any form by any means without the express permission of the author. This includes reprints, excerpts, photocopying, recording, or any future means of reproducing text.

Published in the United States of America by Avalonski Press
ISBN 978-0-9895410-1-5

Do you have a cat . . .

. . . who completely rebuffs your lap?

You've tried bribery.

You've tried insisting.

Nothing works.

Certainly such abnormal behavior requires medical attention.

You take your cat to the vet.

"Oh, no!"

You join a support group.

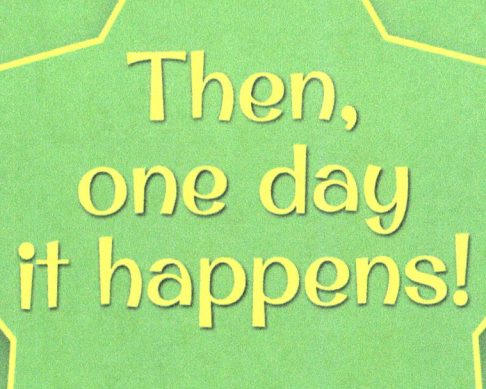

Day after day after day, your cat contentedly sits on your lap.

However, the very unpredictable nature of LRS also means that one day . . .

Stephanie Bouchard
is a journalist and editor. She lives with her lap-reluctant cat, Avalon, the inspiration for this book, and her life partner, Bruce, in Bath, Maine. To contact her, go to stephaniebouchard.net.

Beth Zyglowicz
is an artist, illustrator, and cat-lover based in Indianapolis. She lives with two cats, the shy but friendly Mercutio, and lap-reluctant Beatrice, Princess of Disdain. They both provided ample reference on a range of cat expressions.

www.ingramcontent.com/pod-product-compliance
Lightning Source LLC
Chambersburg PA
CBHW050124020526
44112CB00035B/2465